6:24 pm

so here we are, in between
dreams and death lies life it
seems

so then what does that make us?

i guess strangers in a sea of
strangers, finding meaning

either way my friend, take care

you will see me on the other
side of the evening

poems on offer this evening

this land of

sunsets and giants

OVERTURE

These words are just some
motions from my corner

Neither dogmatic nor a prophecy

And as I fall asleep tonight,
I do so with a reverie

That wherever you wake this
morning, maybe you will think
of me

Those fields of iris amongst
that chalet retreat

From lost angels to devils in
love

We come together, and through
that we learn to fight for peace

I was never taught love

How was I supposed to know to
go to war for it

It was you who gave me that
guidance over drinks

You have to fight for your
health

Like they taught you to fight
for your wealth

You taught me that one in your
backseat

We were phosphenes over the
Lewis River then

Lovers for a night and
confidants for a week

In your eyes, I felt complete

And I could tell you felt the
same

Our faces were mirrors

I could see the blush in your
cheeks

I've seen men on their knees

Praying for something more than
simple charity

Oh please

You speak of a truth only you
can see

Honestly

I would rather cut myself

Than watch you make these
people bleed

It's a fallacy

How they dine on tragedy

And twist the blade until your
smiles turns to pleas

There's no need

Come dawn, we will all be free

Yes indeed

Come dusk, our locks will have
a key

And by tonight, we might even
come together again and finally
feel complete

FOREGARDEN

She was the only good thing to
come out of a wedding in my
twenties

Besides all that other love

First gaze, I swear her eyes
were like movies

Lovely stars, projected some
hurt and fire from within

Transient heat

All of our sentences ended in
a blush

Pink skies

When she danced it was kinetic

Her physique lush

Now I might be a sinner

Only liars say they're not

But her words were a blessing

I asked her what it is she
yearns for

She told me that for now, to
feel seen is enough

I can do that

That night we took to the
pavement

She told me these streetlights
were endless

Pick a corner of the world

You'll find us under them

Addendum

Her poetry defined my summers

She stated her intentions with
a kiss

We danced under those
streetlights

Our opus

She told me in heaven only
perfect things exist

Down here in this land of
sunsets and giants is where we
belong

She came in for a hug

Delivered a whispered letter

It was addressed to my heart

A question

8

If I had this time

This thing we call time

Would I spend it with her and
watch the party die?

Romance at night we can turn
our screams into harmonies

And we did

We lived this way till the
ground met the leaves

We swam above the poverty line

Put our dreams to the side

Our only reward was a thought

If this is freedom, I could use
a little less

A little more comfort

A little less stress

When it became too much, she
came to me with thoughts in hand

Since we have time

This thing we call time

Would you like to turn our
boredom into crime?

We stole from the giants

Turned it back to the folk

An analog cowgirl and a digital
cowboy

Pushing forward while trying to
heal from our past lives

In a world big on sharing the
wrong things

She always asked to hear the
right ones

And they would tell her

Quietly she held the weight of
all our sorrows

All while holding her own

Yet that smile always remained

Oh how your knees must shake

To hold all our sorrow

Comedy might be our last line
of defense

And you're a better comic than
me

I mean I smile for a moment too

But then feel guilty the next

The past won't let me rest

It hounds me, says I'm no better
than my regrets

I ignore it, put my arms across
her chest

I told her if we had this time

This thing we call time

The sun hasn't set yet

Fuck it, let's run it back one
more time

Your diatribe is your own

They can't take that from you

Your cadence

Your speeches

You were always my leader

I guess that's why god needed
you back

She was taken from me deep into
winter

I guess I shouldn't be selfish
the world lost her that morning

And from that day forward my
free time lost the war to
mourning

We didn't even hold a memorial
until spring

Then a little party on the edge
of summer

Attendance of us still living

A requiem from me to you

It was there

Late last June

That she came out of love

For a hug

And I've lived in her arms ever
since

My conversations with her
became my new home

They filled the cracks that
your absence left

Normalcy in a world feeding on
chaos

And my bowl is running low

With time

This thing we call time

These days become years and
these years become days

The seasons blur

We still converse

Yet I fade

I stare into her eyes knowing
she sees the future

She stares into my eyes not
knowing I'll remain in the past

At night the bottle becomes my
muse

The earth's open palms grab at
my back

It takes me under its blanketed
trap

As I fall I have one last answer

I guess if we had this time

Oh this thing we call time

I wouldn't change a thing
because it led me to you

Till our next conversation

Soon

PORT AUTUMN

As I lean on her shoulder

The city in the distance always
looks better to me

The horizon offers hope to a
fiend

It's once you get somewhere
that hope starts to leave

Replaced with something else

A reverie

Her sunburned hair hangs over
me, fallen leaves and lust

A tragedy

Follow the power lines and tell
me what do you see

A city resting in the distance

Dipped in the glow of moonlight
and sunbeams

Flowing endlessly

Just remember that hope and
horror are a two sided coin

And not all of us can forget
how to breathe

So don't be afraid to fall
in love with that city in the
distance

Just don't also forget how to
leave

SAINT ELLA

Would I fall trap to the prey
of another?

Then later that night, crawl
into the bed of a lover

Could the candle dying in her
room represent my passions

And as we lay there together,
I watched us burn

Ashes into ashes

Should the kiss of defeat

Taste this sweet

If it comes from the one
who's dropping body bags on the
concrete

Oh Saint Ella

We wake with pleasures borrowed

Fresh with sorrow

And with the grief of the dying
light

We face the morrow

THIS LAND OF SUNSETS AND GIANTS

I

This land of sunsets and giants

This lukewarm land of love and hate

This game of egos

This ravine of purpose and pace

This place of privilege and character

Of moments and fate

Of the earth that greets us outside our homes

Of the beauty she creates

This land of horror and temptation

Of fallen poets and dying celebration

To the mother who just wants to trust

And the father who will die trying to understand her

This land of sunsets and giants

It won't let us rest

It's endless with or without us

So take a breathe

II

And savor that, we'll cap it
here

Long is the night, and early is
the year

Grab hold of that knife, plunge
it into your fears

Or here's my shoulder if you
need to relinquish some tears

For tomorrow is tomorrow, and
the day is the past

This thing we call time will
never let you last

But that's not the now, hold
off your sorrow

Just take my hand, for we got
tomorrow

I mean look at us

22

We're all young gradients still finding our hue

I know you're hurt, I feel it too

Going forward from here you're going to hold onto some pain

It will devour you whole if you let it stay

Give it someone to talk to, give it some grace

Let it form the man you are today

She told me to find peace in the interludes

They haven't seen the clouds through your eyes

So create your own mantra

Get to work, cut the seams and the internal lies

Find a god or a vice

Just remember everything has a price

She handed me a drink

She said savor that, we'll cap it here

Long is the night, and early is the year

Grab hold of that knife, plunge
it into your fears

Or here's my shoulder if you
need to relinquish some tears

For tomorrow is tomorrow, and
the day is the past

This thing we call time will
never let you last

But that's not the now, hold
off your sorrow

Just take my hand, for we got
tomorrow

AGAINST THE HILL

Clouds foam in the blue above

As I stare at the water I
reflect on love

Oceans into oceans, my friends

Have we all just come here, come
to die?

Motions into motions then

I will thrive in pretend

The freeway reminds me the
world still moves

And that even dreaded constants
can learn to survive

I've given my knowledge to the
young

Will I die in a staring contest
with the sun?

Or will all the people I've come
to love

Come to die?

Against the hill I'll live my
life

Powerlines like ribbons cross
the skies

We live in a reactionary world
you know

And from our leaders, children
learn to lie

What's the truth in all of this

Can a soul learn to persist

Potion sipping potions again

Is everyone just products of
their time

Against the hill I'll die my
love

Is the fading sun a reflection
of us

And have we all just truly come
here, come to die?

THE CALLAWAYS

Have you ever paused
And watched a memory unfold
You're in it now
Yet you know you're going to
miss it when you're old

The Callaways gather around the
LCD
Watching
Reflecting
Listening

Dale R pets Little Miss
Sipping some red wine
Illiam lounges on the sofa
Just counting the time
Andrea lays on the couch
Scout across her lap
And I'm in there somewhere
observing all that

Against the hill
They chose to live their life
Until eventually
Illiam chose to leave us

Maybe he saw something
Something we just couldn't
forsee
Even as his textures begin to
fade with time

Wherever he is at
His smile always seems to
find my mind
And time
like the river it's equal
Flows silently
in the background
Yet aligned

LAMBS

like lambs to a slaughter
this youth is wasted on me

take this wool back father
time can't echo belief

i watch halcyon sunsets
color the bedroom window with
moonbeams
paradoxical visuals don't
match what i think

in a haste i take this wool
in a daydream i craft a coat
and in a moment of
vulnerability
i wrap it around her vividly

watching monsters
making people bleed
i've been there
i'm learning now
falling in and out of balance
endlessly

it's only when i've
returned back to you
that i see the wound
i had already stuck the knife
too deep

you were right to find flight
in the summers evening
and i was right to dream

our narratives were strong
together
but stronger apart
an agonizing realization

it's with that motion of
time and distance
that i began
to enjoy the seasons
and it's why this
familiar thought
found it's way back home

that like lambs to a slaughter
this finite youth
is wasted on me
and maybe that's the reason

MOSS

beauty is age, lovely moss
among fresh rocks

yet, have i failed?

because the moment we begin to
define beauty for someone else

is that not the moment beauty
is lost?

CHAPTERS BABY, CHAPTERS

Can I fucking speak??

Sitting out over the bay

Wondering, if it's me??

And would I die for peace??

On the drive home

Thinking, what's the point of
getting clean

Figure it out

Smoke him out

Then make him lose his speech

Chapters baby, chapters

It's the pages in between

Running these checks up

Show them who's the queen

Chapters baby, chapters

Of course I bookmark the
moments where you make me feel
sweet

When we come together

It's laughter baby laughter

Your presence is all I ever need

No more alabaster disasters

From the reflections of the
water I find comfort

And I think with you I could
end this life with relief

FILMS

I remember you told me being a
girl is hard

And to explain to you would be
even harder

Then you took my hand and showed
me your favorite films

And perspectives blurred within
the hour

You said and how about being a
man

I said there are two lives

The salt and stone of everyday
me

And the reverie I fantasize

Still there's a quiet rage in
men

And maybe in everyone

An honest devastating
loneliness

Learning to tame it has been
the tradegy of my time

So I shared with her some of my
favorite songs

And by dusk, we had no more
reason to lie

Binding ties formed by the
creations of the mind

Honest conversations over
perspectives we'll never fully
realize

LIKE YOU WOULD GOD

Is that trust even possible?
Are human beings meant to
meld?
Could you tell me your secrets
And talk to me like you would
God?
Forever forming
Forever held
Could you return to me like a
dream?
Can I give you my good
thoughts?
Covered in trust
Can I pen them in ink?
And write to you like I would
god?

He may not like it
That for some it's for no one
This gradient of desire
And for others
Lust is part of you
Like it is me
Forever forming
Till our hearts retire

LIBERTINE

I yearn to drown tonight

In the sheets of another

Linen palms

Bodies used to warm each other

In this piece of mind, time
doesn't stutter

It doesn't haunt or reflect

It simply passes through the
summer

Honest comfort

Pure sublime

Small values

Petty Crimes

We're lost sailors, on the
ocean floor of reason

If you're in accord

Then let us wonder tonight

IN THE SPIRIT OF ALCOR

in the spirit of alcor

a moth floats through the
flames

showing us he doesn't feel pain

but he does

and the auditorium watches him
burn

without reason

without name

SAGE TOWERS

"If I died tonight would I
wake up tomorrow sad about
yesterday"

These were the thoughts of a
lonely Garden Frog

A lonely Garden Frog who
resided in the Sage Towers

He had just finished his drink

Sake on the side

Joined by his good friends

Worm, Mantis, and Hummingbird

They drank to a new chapter

Except this new chapter felt
alot like the last one

"Every day I hop closer to
death," he said

"So what are you going to do
about it?" returned Hummingbird

He responded in kind

"Tonight I'm going to dream, and wherever that dream takes me will be my destination"

And so he slept

And that slumber led to a dream

In this dream he rested on a beach, a sword in his hand

He felt the presence of his friends on the sands

And as the sun began to die, a fresh fear took his heart

It filled him with true horror

The worst life has to offer playing out in his head

Frog awoke with a jolt and hopped to his friends

"I'm going to leave the backyard" he exclaimed

"Somewhere out there is an aurora of a beach, and it's not complete until I've been there. I'm heading out at the earliest"

"No you're not" said Mantis

She rose

"Not without us"

As she smiled, she grabbed all
of our belongings

I'm going to be honest with you
it wasn't much

And then the four heroes
embarked on their journey

What they were honestly trying
to find, I don't even think they
knew

Purpose maybe?

The further they removed
themselves from the Sage Towers

The more Frog hopped with
hesitation

But he always fell back down to
that comfortable earth

It is here that I should note

**That the following information
comes as the memories of a dying
worm**

**So it comes to you as it comes
to me**

Scattered but honest, I think

I know we scaled over the
Giant's Treen, climbing took
days

We floated down the night
rapids with friends of Mantis

We camped out in the crevices
of termites

We watched the horizon erupt in
color and die again

It was a peaceful jaunt till
then

It was the following evening
that we were attacked in the
night

And our fable turns fearful

She faught fearlessly

But it was in this night that
Mantis was killed

And Hummingbird's wing was
almost severed by blade

I cry writing this part

Frog and Hummingbird stayed up
all night tracking down the
killers

The perpetrators did not see
the colors rise

And that night the Sage Towers
four became three

The following morning we buried
Mantis

I thought about turning back

I know Frog wanted to return
home

It was Hummingbird, wing almost
apart who told us we march forth

We didn't see it there, but she
was right

II

In a test of incredible courage
and resilience

Hummingbird gave us travel to
the land below

We held on to her back

What an incredible friend she
is

She flew us through the clouds
and past the edges of the treen

It was the next chapter I recall
fondly

As we descended through the
clouds

It was there my eyes came across
the City on the Water Lilies

Mantis would have shed tears of
joy if she could have seen it

Frog said as much

As we touched down

We were received by a moth named
Hugh

Oh poor Hugh, you did not
deserve your fate my friend

Regardless that arrives later

I will tell you what he told me
that night

Here they worshipped a Heron

This Heron often visited the
waters they called home

The Heron never hunted them, no
it would simply land nearby

The ripples would shake the
city, but nobody would mind

They would run to the twig rails
to watch it land and hunt

One night the three of us walked
through the city

Moving from water lily to water
lily as one does

We felt the water around us
tremble when the Heron decided
to make a landing

And as the Heron hit the surface

We braced for the sound of a
body hitting the pavement

We instead found ourselves
watching a Heron land
gracefully as if in a prepared
dance

The city clapped in kind

It was a show to these folks

Nature playing out as it should

As the Heron kneeled to drink
from the water

It was there we come to our next
point of conflict

You see Garden Frog swore the
Heron looked right at him

The Hummingbird swore they
looked at her

And I the Worm will you the
honest truth

No, they looked at all of us

In fact I say it was at that
moment, on the water, that all
of us defined our own purpose

In fact, I will tell you it now,
as I would tell my friends to
their face

Garden Frog was to travel and
experience the world, dying
once he reached his final
resting place, wherever he
deemed it to be

Hummingbird's was to make a
flight from the Sage Towers all
the way to this supposed Beach,
even with her injured wing

Oh and also write her memoir

And myself

Well I simply needed something
to do

One night, as I watched Frog
and Hummingbird stand near
one another on the balcony.
Hummingbird took her wing and
wrapped it around him

And I pondered the title of my
own story

A light caught my eye, deep in
the sky

I watched it's burning aura
grow larger

It behaved like a star as it
flew across the space above

That was until it began to drop

The city collectively grew
intrigued by the light in the
sky

We all stood now, watching
as the flame grew closer and
closer

Until it was revealed

The ball of flame and burning
flesh was not a star

But the dying Heron

We came together and watched
them drop

The impact shook the city,
flames scattered across the
ocean surface

Before he could see if the Heron
was even still with us

Garden Frog went to avenge them

He hopped in the water and made
his way to the shore with a
speed I only saw one other night

The night we lost Mantis

I went to follow, but was
stopped by Hummingbird's grace

"He will find the source of
the damage, we must aid the one
hurting"

Hummingbird picked up a nearby
chestnut bucket in her talons

and began to drop water on the
burning and bleeding creature

I slithered at a speed that you
will just have to take my word
for was incredibly quick

I gathered Hugh and whoever
else I could and made for the
orchard boats

As we floated across the
ripples, I watched feathers
engulfed in navy and crimson
flames fall to the waves

Someone did this

And that someone was facing
their reckoning in the form of
a wrathful Garden Frog

You'll have to excuse me on this
next part

I'm not fond of violence

And neither is my memory

I know that they ambushed us
there, right on the waves

Friends of the fiends who
attacked the Heron

We were the target, the Heron
was the distraction

It was here Hugh lost his life
too

But not before he almost
took down every one of those
bastards

I watched him as he flew amongst
the flames and fury

Above the blood and water

His sewing needle dagger in
hand, he sliced his foes
through the night

Then found a rock on the distant
shore to find his eternal sleep

Frog meanwhile continued his
quest for revenge

Following from where the Heron
flew led him up a river and into
the dark forest of many trees

It was here he found what he
sought

A Fox, wearing the armor of a
king and the mask of a killer,
sat on a raised stump

"You who seeks adventure in a
land you were not invited, it
brings problems. We deal with
them tonight"

She removed a blade from the
bark and looked to the Frog,
she had been waiting for him

Just like in the lake, the Heron
was a lure

She told the Frog that she had
the same dream as him

And that in her eyes, there can
only be one hero

"We are truth sayers you and I,
except there can only be one
truth. And I decide it."

And so Frog picked up his sword

And they dueled until the dawn

Atleast that is what Frog told
me

He said his life had come close
to ending many times

After the battle on the water,
Hummingbird grasped me in her
talons and we searched the
forest

We found a pool of blood first,
leading to Frog's arm

The Fox was lying dead beside
it

And over against the same rock
the Fox was once standing on,
now lied Frog

Hummingbird patched him up

Her and Frog rested their heads
against one another

Then he picked up his good sword
with his good arm and hopped

And we followed, what else were
we to do

We walked in silence for a time

The Fox had told Frog something
in her dying words

An impossibly dark cave leads
to a heavenly beach

"You're almost there"

As the doubt in my mind reached
it's peak

Hummingbird heard the sound of
rushing water

And Frog found a cave

When we entered, the darkness
was so vast we didn't know if
we were still alive

That was until a distant
lantern gave us light

It was a man on a boat

A large skeletal man draped in
a cloak

He led us through the river
under the cave on his little
boat

His name was Albear

He said our plight rowed him to
us

In our short time Albear and
I grew to be quite good
acquaintances

I adored the conversation

But the growing sound of
rushing water paused our words

Before I could even thank him,
the waterfall got us first

We fell

And Albear remained at the top
in his boat

He waved to me as the currents
took us

We floated down the river and
through the cave

And onto our new home

A beach

As we came out onto the sands
soft as clouds, we watched it

The colors rised once again

It was here that Frog broke

The loss of mantis, missing
home, the beach he so
desperately seeked

We asked him if this was it

He told us yes

And it was on that beach we
lived out the rest of our days

III

It took practice runs to get
there

But when we missed our friends
back home, Hummingbird would
fly us to the Sage Towers

She would wake up early every
morning to do a run there, she
would return before Frog even
woke and croaked

We always had the Sage Towers

I didn't realize what a
privilege that was

Having a home to go back too

Ever since I wrote that
sentence I never took it for
granted again

Frog continued to travel the
world, or his world

The world available to him I
should say

He continued to be a hero,
whatever that meant to him

One evening, when the sun was a
cream color and the water it's
mirror

Hummingbird and I found Frog
on the shoreline soaked in the
water

He was dying

It was real

He knew it too

That night he died in
Hummingbird's feathers

And he revealed that this beach
was not the beach he saw in his
reverie

No it was just some beach

But after the grief and
the conflict, he needed that
feeling of home

And so it was

And it was for some time

Until that night when the Sage
Towers three became two

We gave him to the Heron the
next morning

Years passed as we lived out
our days on the beach

Frog's death inspired
Hummingbird to begin writing
her memoir

I helped her with the prose

The Worm and the Bird we called
ourselves

One morning I began to grow
worried when she never returned
from her flight to the towers

After much hesitation due
to insecurities and fear, I
decided to go out after her

It took me weeks to get there,
but I knew where I was going

The City on the Water Lilies

Our good friend Albear gave me
a ride when he saved me from a
pack of crossbow welding deer

He had created a special
pavilion for me on his back,
he had anticipated this very
moment he said

He took me to the city, and
together we found her

She lay alone on a water lily
in the pond

Watching the Heron

She had promised not to go until
I found her

I asked her why not tell me
where she was going

She said that her whole life she
could have hidden from whoever
she wanted

She wanted someone to want to
find her

She thanked me for doing that,
as well as our fluctuating
relationship over the years

She thanked Albear for getting
me there

Then she thanked Mantis for
getting us here

And finally she thanked Frog

She believed she was going to
see him soon. I will never know
if she was granted this wish

She passed on that lily pad

We pushed her towards the Heron

The pad floated for awhile

And the following sight I
promised is the whole truth

The Heron picked her up and
carried her away

To go be with Frog

Or atleast that's what I tell
myself

Albear and I returned to the
beach

He never left my side again

We thrived on that beach

We still do to this day

One day I will go

So will Albear

And our story would be over

And what a beautiful ending it
would be

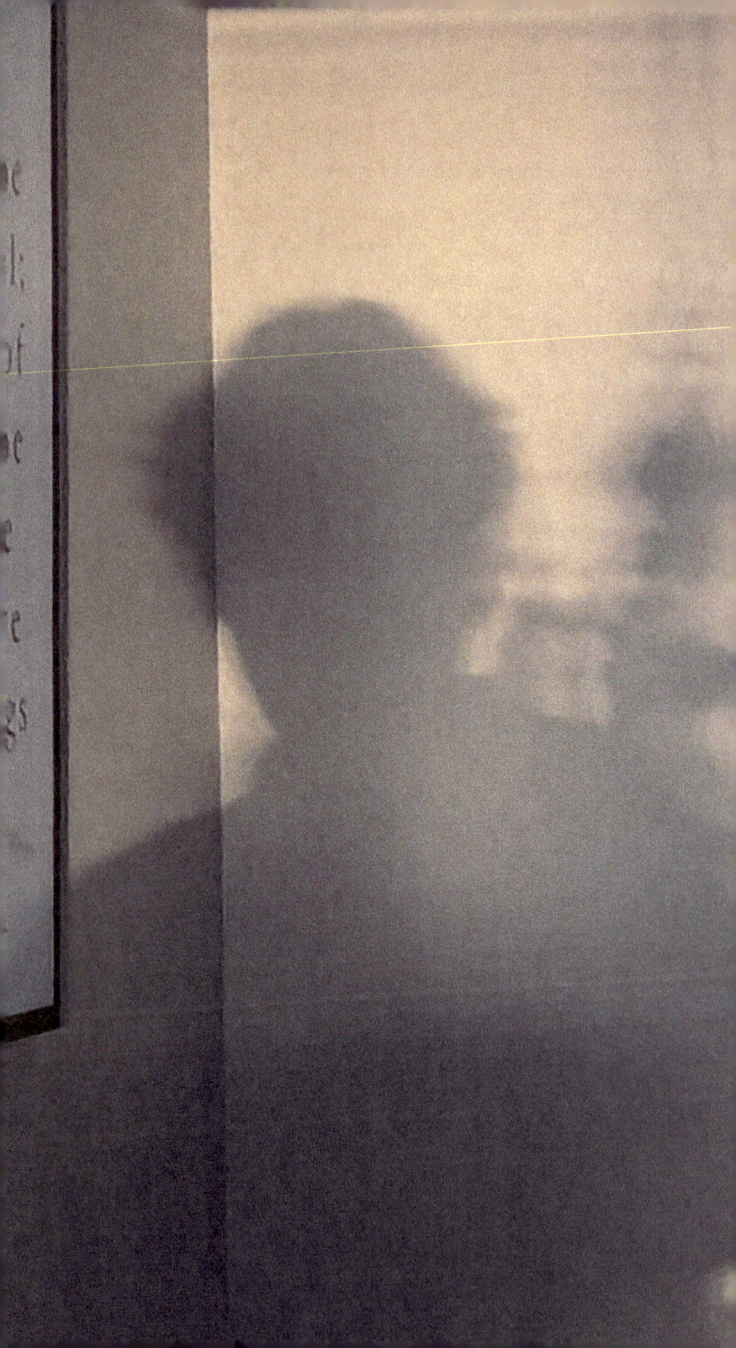

A BLUEPRINT FOR COWARDS

I have made it far enough into
this life to know those without
a spine

The one who touts their cards
instead of putting them on the
line

You present yourself as
strength, to disguise the
snakes that lie in wait

Using religion to mask your
face

And easy lies to form your base

I watch the screen, see venom
dripping from your every word

You're the very thing I have
grown to hate

I've made mistakes and had the
privilege of love and space

Some may call me a coward, but
not today

I had to converse with my
reckoning

And learn to live with my fate

Don't tempt with those vipers,
that's a war I've already faced

Even the moon judges you with
light from above

As your sons attempt to learn
empathy from your hugs

You treat our country's
presence as water to a plant

But we're mother bear

Our children screech for help,
our leg is in a trap

You think you know what makes
us great?

You and your greatness come
from stolen money

Even your very influence is
fake

These words are a blueprint for
all cowards

The ones who can but don't have
the care to change

Whose values disappear when an
innocent light is held to them

Like your very foundation,
opaque

LIGHT FOOTFALL

Buttermilk bitches the lot of
ya

Seriously, you continue to
elude any sense of being
sensible

It's simple

If you yearn for war, then I
yearn for war with you

Seriously, what is the point of
your life if I take it?

Snatching purposes with these
hands

That's what I do

Petty rage lives inside me

And at who?

The world hurts enough it can't
be her

It has to be you

Oh you don't have a soul?

Not my problem

The actions you make though?

Now that's conscious

And it's true

I'm blue

Still finding colors I once
dismissed around the room

I get that we all fall on our
path to the future

Like you

I didn't mean to be ignorant

I was growing seeing the world
from my corner

I was in the paint learning what
it means to find power

What it means to be a man and
dance with the boundaries of
this land

I was new to everything beside
me

It's true

I'm still blue

And still finding colors I once
dismissed around the room

Learning to remove the things I
put in my way

Light footfall in a pale
afternoon, what can I say

Learning to live with the
qualities my parents graced

In our bones their love and hate
is laced

Why do you think I'm writing to
you so soon?

We were always going to come
back to you

I mean think of how much we
don't know

Then think of how little you do

Tell me do you recall your steps
the last time you saw the moon?

Because that is your legacy

Forgotten noise

Just some petty footfall around
the room

REGICIDE

It's a regicide

And guess what, all the kings
are outside

Swap the vices

And darling lover of many
triumphs

Come settle by

The world outside my comfort
scares me

And these flowers are looking
mighty fine

So slither tides

A season of change will soon be
blowing by

And I'm terrified

If you would have me

I would have you endlessly into
night

Because, these lies I tell
myself have me petrified

I've lost this love for the life
that I lead

I know longer know if the change
that I want is the change that
I need

That's why I feel you slipping

And I no longer understand what
it means to succeed

The compass that got me off the
rocks has now left me on the
shore

And it was in that moment

Those thoughts of reflection
didn't just drip they poured

I wondered

How many pathethic poems can
one man make

I don't know, I stopped
counting and kept writing after
eight

Because America is a two-sided
coin, hope and horror

While in the corner

Doomed giants play dice with
gods

And we romanticize the sunsets
to escape our fates

Always pushing us from bliss to
bleakness

Flawed men's eternal weakness

So now it's a regicide

And guess what, all the kings
are outside

Swap the vices

And darling lover of many
triumphs

Come settle by

The world outside my comfort
scares me

And these flowers are looking
mighty fine

So slither tides

A season of change will soon be
blowing by

And honestly I'm okay tonight

Because if you would have me

I would have you endlessly

And what then my dear, what
could we fear but time?

FLORENCE

Fall short of a fallen breath

It's you who cuts the seams

The only enemy of eternity

She came to me in a reverie

Then again in the spring

And the fear that boiled in my
blood went with her

I found our conversation to
give me life

She must have felt the same

Because she laid with me until
winter

We used our bodies for warmth

And our voices to see how we're
doing

That was until the summer, when
she left and took me with her

Where we went I promised I would
not say

But if anyone still asks about me

Tell them I'm okay

Through the summer haze

Autumn's sol was just lying there

So in the winter chill, we lay there bare

We spring back to life when the rain hits

Two strangers turned lovers behaving like kids

It was a fallacy built upon a dream going out like a lamb

So when we came together, it didn't feel real

And when you left I couldn't understand

And I'm sorry for that

I couldn't understand

Burns from that night kept me out of the room for days

I began to mourn the way you moved, all your endemic ways

Florence the power you hold

It ignited a war that lay
dormant just behind my face

And I couldn't understand

I'm sorry for that

I couldn't understand

On the otherside of autumn

As the conversation ended in
your front seat

You looked to me

And I to you

And somewhere in the silence we
found an understanding

PALACE BEFORE

Tonight, I come to you for
warmth

So we can dream of a palace
before

We were still grieving your
innocence

Now it's the rest of you we have
to mourn

So no more questions, please

See, my brother died today can
I get some peace

Just for one day can I not plan
out my future

Can I exist in the past, set up
a little shelter there

Maybe die for a few months, come
alive when the time is right

See, because people said pray
and the prayers led me here

With my head in my hands and my
heart full of fear

They told my brother the same thing

Are we praying to the same end?

I know how much easier it is to believe

But when butterfly wings can turn to halos

Shouldn't we question?

You know what, no more

From now on I perform

And retreat to the palace before

I see now
That they can't take my dreams

That this morning was simply a wave going back out to sea

That these days of grief are a bridge

Forevers remedy

And lord knows I can't see it now

But the moment my brother went from a moment to a memory

Was also the day I went from who I was

To who I'm going to be

TO RUST

Oh I'm searching
Searching for something
Saying shit I don't know
Either way here we go

Playin
Playin to a beat
I don't know the notes, and I
certainly don't like how it's
been treatin me

Fallin
Fallin back a step
If this is the end of my time
I guess at least it's an end

Watchin
Watchin everything take a
breathe
And I just know it's coming
The pain of reality
Dear lord
If you're out there watchin
Please watch over me

Say it
In the tone of love
It's been far too long since
I've had an honest hug

This rust
It's made its way to the bone

But I'm here still
Till my name is in stone

To rust
To breathe
To love
To death
To steps
To mistakes
To learn the most, one can take

To rust
To fear
To life
Hold me dear
I'm here
Stay there
I'll be home soon
To repair
So take head
Because now I see what it takes
To rust
To rust

To rust

To rust

SOMEONE BLURRY COMES THIS WAY

It's all blurring together

Living

Surviving

and Thriving

Don't think I haven't forgotten
the enemy though

Dying

You instilled that in me

Before I knew that meaning and
purpose came together

I hadn't yet defined what gave
me pleasure

I hadn't yet found what gave me
pain

No one taught me how to love

I learned that one through
mistakes

I watched a distant mother
ignore her child

And I learned what it is to hate

What it is to put a mask over
your face

And learn to love before it's
too late

At dusk

Someone blurry comes this way

They ask to know what I've
learned

And if it's going to be okay

We swapped irises

And I was honest with them

That this life shit is a work
in progress

That learning isn't a battle

It's a never-ending conquest

Until your knees fall at the
feet of death

And she takes you away into the
clouds

Coiled around her breast

Even then your biggest enemy
came to be a friend

You could not define your foes

You could not define a trend

So I guess I'll keep falling
until I fall back in love

Or until my heart retires and
my future undun

Blurry faces

Blurry days

As I march through these
moments, I'm reminded of fate

Blurry thoughts

Blurry touches

At dusk

Someone blurry comes this way

She wears many masks and hold
many names

And as we walk back together
from whence she came

I see now it's always been you

So I stand blushing in your
presence

Realizing why before I never
had the right words to make
someone stay

And how the best and worst
people in my life

Were all once someone blurry
just coming this way

CARPETFACE

I saw a face in the carpet
and everything started talking
you see

The walls started blurring
as my friends all moved
further
away from me

"I promise not to lose them."
Wait I said that once before
It was before you lost
another one, and after you had
already lost a few more

Attempting to escape
this thought
Is when I awoke
on that unknown boat
To a skeletal man
draped in a shadowy cloak

He gently took my hand, would
you like to know what he said?

He got real close and said
"my name is Albear, and I give
guidance to the dead"

He told me it was conversation
That was his favorite teacher
Something we used to
have in common
"Learn from this ride" he said

"I know I have"
See apparently he's been rowing
folks ever since he was thought
to exist

We traveled down a river
It's chemistry composed
of darkened waters
I asked him where we're going
and he just put his hand
on my shoulder

I watched as he rowed us onward
toward a cave, the entrance a
shaded wall
The sound of rushing water
slowly growing loud
The hope in my stomach
beginning to fall

A drop kind of like Pirates, a
themepark ride to the lost
I turned to the man
looking for some hope
He said nothing

Yet he had faced this once
before
You could see it on his face
That was it, that was what I
needed
So I clutched onto the sides
We pushed into the darkness
From it the souls of the damned
cried and cried

The boat tipped over
Down into the black
I didn't scream
I didn't falter
I braved the rising sun
And as I fell down the

waterfall
The darkness became my home

My thoughts became my own

And the dream becomes a tome

That's what it does when it
dies
I seem to appreciate the
dreams
more after they die
As I awake to that
familar ceiling
Face to face with that familar
room
I look down to the carpet

And there is no face to be seen

INTERLUDES

I'm not picky with my
meditations

I mean just ask the monk down
the street

We nodded to him in silence

As you and I pursued flowers
with the drink

Explored valleys through gentle
touch

And exchanged vows with our
bodies linked

Sweet benediction on the
evening after summer

I always knew I never left the
house for a reason

Discovering how the world falls
back into familiar patterns

And how I hurt those I believed
in

Kept me shadowed in shelter

Living in interludes

Merely an observer of her
seasons

BASIL

I

Heard them talking down the
hall

They said when god created the
earth he did so at night

The dawn of the first day
happened at dusk

Maybe that's why I haven't been
to church in fifteen years

I was never meant to be up

So what?

I'm up now

And I'm convinced the things
keeping me here will never be
found

In ignorance, I'd rather drown

In the regrets of the many
before my own

So please just pick up the phone

I have breaking news, we were
never meant to be alone

It's why we get stoned

Benevolent poison pills keeping
the marrow in the bone

You rolled the flowers in the
vase and became my home

II

So darling lover
Fall back again
Then fall into me
Grasp my hand
Then take this peace

Oh I'm scared for us
Look how far we've come
And how much further
until we've won
Sense the tone
Then sense the fear
Oh my lord
My time is near

Fuck the fallen
Not the ones who have gone
But the ones still here
Hurting the world from
their thrones

I've been afraid, for oh so
long
But as tonight beckons
so will the dawn

And as I read these
words to you
I do so as a song
So when you wake this morning
it is then you will see
That I have left a light on
in the clouds for you
and when I'm gone
all I ask is that you
please keep our forest lit for
me

SEPTEMBER

If desire was to be
And to yearn was wanting more
Have you ever felt these
sorrows
And still been numb to it all?

Always seeking the warmth of
another
Yet wouldn't allow myself her
touch

I was lost in my own salvation
Yearning for some kind of lust
Some kind of life
Some kind of love

So as I marched through this
time

A libertine still forming
from night to night

A despond
from October's fall

A blight
to August's light

It was only in September's rest

That I learned loneliness is a
true enemy of us

NORTH FROM HERE, NORTHSTAR

North from here, Northstar

Your steps have grown scared

I write from the shadows cast
by my past

Maybe you can take some of it
and take care

Those moments in bed when
you're afraid for tomorrow

Those moments when ashes of
past lights

Ignite the current fires of
despair

Go North from here, my
Northstar

Get out of the furnace while
you can

I've lost brothers to
themselves

I've lost sisters to the grief

And as I stood above their
graves, it was there I could
see

That we face an end whether or
not you're on your knees

And I prefer to stand and face
the breeze

Go North From Here, my darling
Northstar

Get out of this town while you
can

I sing songs of love and death

To try to bring something to
this land

Most days I wonder if it's
nothing to them

But if it's something to you

Then maybe we can come together
and pretend

HOSPICE

A small code and we're in
To the place where people go to
lie
I find a seat beside her
My parents rest on the other
side

She gives us a list of those who
should know where she goes
Picked up the phone and found
out they had already left
I told her so
She stared into my eyes with
regret

So this is growing old she said
So this is what it means to rest
on epoch's knife
She looks to the gown resting
in the closet
Her final evening attire

A blessing and blight this is
To make it to this moment
From caretaker to taken care
of
The epilogue of life

LORD OF THE MARIGOLDS

I've been lost in my head
I've been gone for days
And when people ask me how I
am
I just don't know what to say

Lord of The Marigolds please
come take me away

I've been walking around
In heavy conversation
with clowns
Living downtown
just for the sounds

I was moving South
Falling from the East
I arose in the West
And I just couldn't compete
So I settled in the North, and
lived my life on repeat

Lord of The Marigolds we've
come close and still we've
failed to meet

Instilled with a nomads truth
meant with time I had to move
Friends letting friends loose
is never an easy truth

"Leave us some advice"
So this ballad was lent
I told them I was just here

for the clowns
And these days my smiles are
spent

Without laughter, without
light
These concrete cities
are just pillars of plight
So farewell my friends
If it's there
I'll see you in the next life

So I took my past and my pride
and left my legacy with my dog
I boarded the train to forever
I wanted you to think of me
when you looked to the stars
And as I found my seat
The Lord of the Marigolds
found me
And an absolute fear took my
heart

"Could you use someone for the
ride ahead?"
He found his seat next to mine
And as I sat in solace
for another lonely journey
I looked back on the fragile
life I had left behind

In shame, I turned to his eyes
"I could" I said
If you want someone to share
your heart
it can't begin with a lie
And from that moment
forever more
On this train to a future eden

It was the
Lord of the Marigolds and I

GOTHIC

Should we start with how you
were immaculance defined

And how it was your poetry that
defined my summers

Our bodies entwined

Somehow under the hues of
moonlight we both remember
sunshine

Our conversations were enough
to keep us happy for both our
lives

Floating by these suburban
castles

The streetlights were our
stagelights

The moonlight the highlight

Esoteric hearts melting
esoteric minds

You viewed your existence as a
crime

And I never knew why

Until I did

Digital love met digital
disdain

We were both hurt, our souls
topped with analog pain

Fear and anxiety kept my heart
in sobriety

And the flowers kept my blood
in their veins

Arms around a trauma I told
myself I beat

Isolation fed desperation, what
was feeding me?

Gothic in nature
I hope you can find your reason

Lost in fear
afraid to make a move

Because
I've only now noticed the
pattern

Everytime I do
I lose you too

VIDEO DREAMS, DARLING

Among the lucky
i'm the chosen one

A family mantra my brother
wears like a badge

As I write this he's
losing his mom and dad

The softest soul I know
lost her son to the waves

Whose name will we see
next at the graves

We live in video dreams
darling, video dreams
Death and time are eternal
regimes
In the end
Are we not just leaves in a
stream?

Do you fear what we could
do with eternity?
Or do you spare us
from that burden?

It's not weak to fear death
Either way
the dream ends the same
With the same ceilings above

us
And that familar ground beneath

With time,I got pretty good at
dreaming
By twelve, even had a reverie
of who I wanted to be
My polaroid sunset

But it takes more than a dream
to endure here
I found more comfort in the glow
of a TV
A man can only
imagine himself
the hero so many times
So when I graduated high
school
I saw how i was going to die
My polaroid sunset
Ever since then, a fear has
never left me
and even that was a privilege

Take me back to those video
dreams darling, those video
dreams
Bound by death and time,
eternal regimes
In the end
are we not just pebbles in a
stream?

No, we're also gradients of
color and beauty supreme
And even the worst of us can't
take our daydreams

That's where I find myself now
On the eve of summer
These sunkissed
Cul-de-sac trips
Have become a refuge for a

while
I've done wrong to people and
for that I apologize
I promise I'll spend my
remaining time figuring out why

People are boundaries
to be protected
Mausoleums to learn from
and stories to be projected

On the rocks
against the pavement
I face an honest truth
What we do here matters
And I'm too scared to move

We live in video dreams
darling, video dreams

Death and time are
eternal regimes

In the end
We might just be pebbles
without a purpose

Leaves lost in a stream
Blurry romantic pixels
Left to die on a screen

We all grieve
But knowing someone else
is out there grieving too
And that we can hold each other
Well that might be my only
relief

BLUSH

Here's to twenty-three trips
around the seasons

God, I thought you promised me
twenty more

In the backseat with your hair
over me

The ultraviolet light pours
from the store

Around thirty-one passages to
Venus

Do you count the birthdays
before?

My hand on your thighs

That look in your eyes

It's led me astray before

In that gaze, there's more
anger than love

Yet more passion than rage

You once told me there was
vitriol flowing through your
veins

Caused by a man

Enough to ignite a flame

Cauterize the wound

What follows rage?

Pain

Thirty-six clips in the chamber

Just give me forty seconds more

I love to set the tinder

Set myself ablaze when I'm a
winner

But with you

Well, you settle the score

Twenty-three trips around the
seasons

God give me twenty more

In the ultraviolet night

Gripping you tight

I'll gladly await the morn

MANTRA

Hey hurt one

Now tomorrow might not make it

If we can't learn how to get
through today

Now I know you're busy waiting

Waiting on a dream or a lover
to take you far away

But if we can't get through
tomorrow

How will we tell our kids to
get through today

So tomorrow might not make it

If we can't learn how to get
through the day

SO OUR ERA BEGINS

I

So our era begins

And in an ode, we party like
fools

Nobody warned us though

That in this land of sunsets
and giants

We're all fools

And darling lover of many
triumphs, I was lost around the
room

So in a daze I went looking for
answers

And that's when I came to you

To this woman, adorned in
honest rage on the news

She speaks of a clementine for
your clemency

I hope you cherish the flavor

And as all the sycophants hug
their young ones

They realize every street has a
different beggar

Moments before they shot the
man, they told us they were our
saviors

I see these men with guns
wherever you can read a fucking
paper

If the race was never about
skin, then how come we weren't
taught in the same favor

I'll be fine, what about the
ones who won't

It could be your neighbor

From the starting line, he
drinks his gin

He thinks he'll finish safer

These little men

With grand egos

All traitors

With no choice but to play their
games

Two more children were killed
by a tank

I watched it on the television

One side of the bar screams for
help while the rest just sit
and listen

Momentary bliss

Tomorrow I can already tell you
will seek division

Seek a peace that can tame all
these hungry foxes, the ones
always sifting

I hear a ballad from the man on
the street telling us it's true

As we turn back to the TV from
the romantics, I hear the news

Of those familiar gunmetal cues

On the pavement where they
lived their lives

They now form a symphony of
crimson hues

To the people beside me, how
can that not make you rage?

But I get it

What are we to do?

How about for once you ask the
people in the flames for the
truth

I guess that's why I wrote this

And the powerlessness of it all

If I had to fight for something

I would fight that your next
step is one you can afford

And no matter the hue

Your next dream is one you can
choose

II

And so our era begins

And in an ode, we party like
fools

Nobody warned us though

That in this land of sunsets
and giants

We're all fools

And darling lover of many
triumphs, I've been lost around
the room

So, in a daze I went looking
for answers

And that's when I came to you

This abandoned nomad on the
street

He told me

Maybe your god isn't the great
one if it needs you to make him
real?

That if we chose when we lost
people, would we cherish them
still?

He said, of course ignorance
abounds when you serve it like
pastries

We're all just characters for
the crows

And it's your system that made
me

As my time turns to an an end
and I become revolutionary dust

I ask that you still seek love,
that you fight for your comfort

That's a must

I've rejected emperors and lost
wars

But still, I trust

I trust those who got me here

Which isn't much

He got closer, a few more
questions

Have you met the human?

The one who is covered in
greed, the one who must have
been tricked that winning is
currency

What about the troubled man
who makes both mistakes and
promises?

That is me, sin drips from my
accomplishments

How about the one who used to
walk with both heart and mind?

Her memory keeps me hopeful
when time runs dry

I watched a tear hit the
pavement, followed by a sigh

Then he shook my hand, hugged
me, and then left the city
limits to die

III

So our era begins

And in an ode, we party like
fools

Nobody warned us though

144

That in this land of sunsets
and giants

We're all fools

And darling lover of many
triumphs, I've been lost around
the room

So in a daze I went looking for
answers

And eventually found my way
back to you

A lost man, learning how he can
put his soul to use

I rejected an empress out of
pain and still feel the torment

I found mercy in the form of a
friend

And in my own loneliness I got
too close to her again and again

If my regret can be felt, then
let it be felt here

As I watch the sun rise

The smoke brings warmth to my
fears

An ocean of momentary tears

This dance of flawed and
grieving people raising flawed
and growing children

It's a war, everyone must play
their part you see

And I've played mine

Now it's about time I figure
out the man I outta be

So I'll say farewell whenever
it begins to snow

Don't worry, it always seems to
be winter wherever I go

Still, I watch the summer sun
leave us here to bring the day
to someone else

I watch the tears on the shower
glass become the emotions we
felt

I think back on all of
those limbo nights and the
conversations we held

And how even the aged leaf
ultimately fell

So as our era begins

And in an ode, we party like
fools

Know these words were not just
from me

They were the final words of
the youth

And if we fail

We all go down together

And their legacy like stolen
caskets

Will be engraved on all our
tombs

FREE SMOKE BREAKS

As the leaves hit the shore

We watch the summers die

And those that we walked with
we leave them behind

I see now I must if I'm to make
it to my end

But thank you for getting me
here my friends

Clean leaves leave little
treasures

Those dipped in blood leave
something else

I see now what it takes
to exist within yourself

Grief, it's letting us know
that you are missed

I didn't need the reminder
but thanks for the gift

I survive off
learned behavior now

It's here at home
I'm planting my flag

It's here

I choose to fight my war
alone and through strife

It was here

I learned memories can sting

It was here

I saw the curvature of life

I've loved and lost

And learned the secrets of our
era

So when you go don't ask me how
I know

But there are free smoke breaks
in hell

So take this time to collect
your vices before the funeral

That way when the leaves hit
the shores

And the summers begin to die

When those that we walked with

when it's time to leave them
behind

I see now my dear that we all
face an end

But thanks to the ghosts for
getting me here my friends

I would be lying if I said
I wasn't going to fuck up again

But there's wisdom in youth and
there is wisdom with age

So I give all my love to those
who made me who I am today

And when the time comes for
death and I to become one

I will go like we all do

In both fear and love

12:05 am

i still read it you know,
the book of your poems you
left for me. it was that
and your old camera, that's
all that remained. so just
know i've been taking pictures
with it, and i'll include them
throughout these pages for you
to see

though i think maybe it's time
the world heard from some other
perspetives. so i'll leave the
words with you, and when you
feel it's time for them to be
out in the open, let them free.
it might be selfish, but i want
someone to know i stood on this
earth. that i was here in this
land of sunsets and giants for
just a moment, and i did okay.
so until i can look into your
eyes and speak them myself, i
hope this will remedy where we
left each other, and by tonight
maybe even bring us together

until that day,

take care

Thank you for your time tonight, I wish you wonder in whatever comes next

Besides select poems, This Land of Sunsets and Giants was written throughout the months of January to July in the year 2025.

www.ingramcontent.com/pod-product-compliance
Lightning Source LLC
Chambersburg PA
CBHW071403120626
46546CB00002B/795